GOLFING
Wit

GOLFING WIT

First published in 2007
Reprinted 2008, 2009, 2010, 2011, 2012
This edition copyright © Summersdale Publishers Ltd, 2015

Illustrations © Ian Baker

Aubrey Malone has asserted his right to be identified as the author of this work in accordance with sections 77 and 78 of the Copyright, Designs and Patents Act 1988.

Summersdale Publishers Ltd
46 West Street
Chichester
West Sussex
PO19 1RP
UK

www.summersdale.com

Printed and bound in the Czech Republic

ISBN: 978-1-84953-662-2

Substantial discounts on bulk quantities of Summersdale books are available to corporations, professional associations and other organisations. For details contact Nicky Douglas by telephone: +44 (0) 1243 756902, fax: +44 (0) 1243 786300 or email: nicky@summersdale.com.

GOLFING
Wit

QUIPS AND QUOTES FOR THE GOLF-OBSESSED

AUBREY MALONE

summersdale

CONTENTS

EDITOR'S NOTE

I'm not really gloating at the lovable losers or dotty eccentrics in this volume. They're more like my soulmates in crime, viewed from the relative safety of the 19th (hic!) hole. That's where you can sit over your pint and reminisce quietly about your purgatorial double bogeys as if they were perpetrated by someone else, and fantasise about the dream holes-in-one to a barman who probably won't care if they happened or not.

You can keep to yourself the manifold times you beheaded the ball, or hit your face with the club on your backswing as the divot went higher than a house and you found yourself begging for your fifth mulligan... on the same hole.

When I started this project I wasn't at all sure that the pros could be as (unintentionally) funny as yours truly. Nick Faldo? Bernhard Langer? Pul-eease! Better quote Phil Silvers' line: 'Be funny on a golf course? Do I kid my best friend's mother about her heart condition?'

But yes, dear reader, there was humour to be found, though not always where expected. I could have filled the book on Lee Trevino's expostulations alone but there were other unlikely jokesmiths too. Many of the jokes were rueful, and/or black, as one might be entitled to expect from a game that looks like heaven and feels like hell.

Some people call it terminally boring and others an unconquerable addiction. Somewhere in the middle of this fairway are the walking (and joking) wounded. This is their story.

WHAT IS GOLF?

Golf is the loneliest
of all games, not
excluding postal chess.

PETER DOBEREINER

Golf is somewhere
between making love
and writing a poem.

JOHN UPDIKE

Golf is a game where
white men can dress
up as black pimps and
get away with it.

ROBIN WILLIAMS

Golf is not a funeral, though
both can be very sad affairs.

BERNARD DARWIN

In Africa the natives have the
custom of beating their clubs
and uttering blood-curdling
yells. Anthropologists call
this a form of self-expression.
In Europe we call it golf.

PHIL SILVERS

Golf is a game where you sock
the ball hard and walk four feet.

HERBERT PROCHNOW

————— •●• —————

Golf should be played on
Sunday, not being a game in
the view of the law, but rather
a form of moral effort.

STEPHEN LEACOCK

————— •●• —————

Golf was never meant
to be an exact science.
Einstein was lousy at it.

BOB TOSKI

The game was invented
for simpletons.

SPIKE MILLIGAN

WHERE IT ALL BEGAN

I sometimes wonder
how they survived
my childhood!

JACK NICKLAUS ON HIS MOTHER AND SISTER

The best year of my life was when
I was 11. I... won 32 tournaments.
Everything's been downhill since.

TIGER WOODS

———•••———

Dad, what do people do on
Sunday who don't play golf?

BOBBY JONES TO HIS FATHER AS A CHILD

———•••———

When I first started golf, my
father told me I was going to
do more good than Gandhi,
Mother Teresa, the Pope and
Tony Blair all rolled into one.

TIGER WOODS

As a child, Seve Ballesteros used to chip pesetas into holes. Since then he's been shovelling them into his pockets.

BEN CRENSHAW

———•••———

I'll never play golf. It's a cissy game.

ARNOLD PALMER TO HIS FATHER AT 15

———•••———

My family was so poor, the lady next door gave birth to me.

LEE TREVINO

HIT AND MRS

Although we are
told nothing about
it, there can be little
doubt that one of Job's
chief trials was that
his wife insisted on
playing golf with him.

P. G. WODEHOUSE

They say passion for
golf is a recipe for
mental illness. Logically
speaking, playing
with your wife should
double that danger.

LES DAWSON

I plan to be a golf widow next week. I've just bought the gun.

JOAN RIVERS

———•●•———

My wife and I are doing everything we can to keep our marriage together. We have candle-lit dinners twice a week. She goes Tuesdays, I go Fridays.

WALTER HAGEN

———•●•———

'Mildred, shut up,' cried the golfer at his nagging wife, 'shut up or you'll drive me out of my mind.' 'That,' snapped Mildred, 'wouldn't be a drive. That would be a putt.'

DEBORAH KAYSER

Golf is wrecking my head.
Yesterday I kissed my seven-iron
goodbye and putted my wife.

DON RICKLES

— •●• —

Footballers' wives fall out
of taxis blathered at 3 a.m.
in red-light districts. The
worst a golf wife does is wear
an uncoordinated dress.

SHELLY KIRKLAND

— •●• —

That's what happens when you
haven't been home in 18 years.

LEE TREVINO ON HIS DIVORCE

Give me my golf clubs, fresh
air and a beautiful partner
and you can keep the golf
clubs and the fresh air.

JACK BENNY

———•••———

Our relationship lasted longer
than either of his two marriages.

NICK FALDO'S CADDY DAVID LEADBETTER, WHO
WAS SACKED BY FALDO AFTER 13 YEARS

———•••———

Playing with your spouse on
the golf course runs almost as
great a marital risk as getting
caught playing with someone
else's anywhere else.

PETER ANDREWS

A fanatical golfer is speaking to his friend. 'For years I didn't know where my wife spent her evenings,' he says. The friend asks him how he finally found out. 'Well, one evening I went home and there she was.'

GEORGE BURNS

———————●●●———————

'After all, golf is only a game,' said Millicent. Women say these things without thinking. It does not mean that there is any kink in their character. They simply don't realise what they are saying.

P. G. WODEHOUSE

My wife: You and Jim have
played golf every Sunday for
years. Wouldn't you like to invite
him and his wife to dinner?
Me: Jim is married?

DAVID OWEN

Ladies: If he comes home from the
golf course looking like he's been
at the beach, it's not a good time
to ask him about that new dress.

FRAN LEBOWITZ

My wife doesn't care what
I do when I'm away as long
as I don't have fun.

LEE TREVINO

THE CRUEL GAME

Every time I feel the urge to play golf I go into a corner and put a wet towel over my head until it passes.

SAM LEVENSON

Give me a man with big hands,
big feet and no brains and I
will make a golfer out of him.

WALTER HAGEN

———•••———

I thought about taking up golf...
and then I thought again.

GROUCHO MARX

———•••———

The most maddening thing about
golf is the perversity with which
the body refuses to obey the mind.

PAT WARD-THOMAS

Everyone gets wounded in a game
of golf. The trick is not to bleed.

PETER DOBEREINER

———•●•———

I've been playing golf for
20 years now and have just
made a discovery. I hate it.

REX BEACH

———•●•———

Golf has given me
an understanding
of the futility of life.

ABBA EBAN

I've never been depressed
enough to take up the game.

WILL ROGERS

———•●●•———

I don't want to play golf.
When I hit a ball, I expect
someone else to run after it.

JACKIE GLEASON

———•●●•———

I heard some good news today. Ten
golfers a year are hit by lightning.

GEORGE CARLIN

What is needed instead of all
these instructional books on
how to play golf is a walloping
good book on how to give it up.

MICHAEL GREEN

O. J. Simpson has already
received the ultimate punishment.
For the rest of his life he has
to associate with golfers.

GEORGE CARLIN

Golf is the cruellest of sports. It's
a harlot, an obsession, a boulevard
of broken dreams. It plays with
men and runs off with the butcher.

JIM MURRAY

SLOWCOACHES

Golf teaches us that
although patience is a
virtue, slow play is not.

MARC GELLMAN

The marshal pointed out that we were holding up play so badly, the golfers behind us were building shelters for the night, and the management had set up soup kitchens and group counselling.

MICHAEL PARKINSON

———— •●• ————

Golf is a game in which the slowest people in the world are in front of you, and the fastest ones behind.

KEVIN McCARTHY

———— •●• ————

Ken Brown doesn't need a watch to time himself on a golf course. He needs a calendar.

BUD EGLINTON

The best way to deal with
people hassling you to play
faster is to let them through
– and then hassle them.

JACK BENNY

———————•●●•———————

'What's he waiting for?' said the
spectator as he watched a player
stand motionless over his ball.
His friend replied, 'He's waiting
for the grass to grow up under
it and give him a better lie.'

BOBBY JONES

EXERCISING ONE'S PREROGATIVE

Golf gives you about
as much exercise as
shuffling cards.

BILL COSBY

It looks like a very good exercise, but what's the little white ball for?

ULYSSES S. GRANT UPON SEEING HIS FIRST GAME OF GOLF

———•●•———

At my age I try to work out a little. I go swimming twice a day. It beats buying golf balls.

BOB HOPE

———•●•———

The greatest liar in the world is the golfer who claims he plays the game merely for exercise.

TOMMY BOLT

Arnold Palmer has gone on
a fitness programme. He's
given up cigarettes and started
jogging. He only coughs now
when his opponent is putting.

BING CROSBY

———— •●• ————

Golf teaches us that even
people who wear green pants
deserve some place where they
can go, get a little exercise,
and not be laughed at.

MARC GELLMAN

THE 19TH HOLE

The 19th hole is the only one where players can have as many shots as they like.

LOUIS SAFIAN

What scoundrel took the
cork out of my lunch?

W. C. FIELDS DURING A 'SNACK' BREAK
AT THE LAKESIDE CLUB IN LA

———•••———

A policeman pulled me over
when I had one too many. 'Are
you intending to drive home,
sir?' he asked. 'Well, you don't
expect me to walk in this
condition, do you?' I replied.

DOUG SANDERS

———•••———

Arsenic.

BEN CRENSHAW TO A BARTENDER WHO ASKED HIM
WHAT HE WANTED TO DRINK AFTER HE FAILED TO
QUALIFY FOR THE BRITISH OPEN IN 1992

The bartender in the clubhouse hears so many stories about missed opportunities and failed lives, he could charge analysis fees. He shouldn't put out bar stools. Couches would be more appropriate.

ROBERT POWELL

My favourite hole was
always the watering hole.

RONAN RAFFERTY

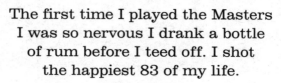

The first time I played the Masters
I was so nervous I drank a bottle
of rum before I teed off. I shot
the happiest 83 of my life.

CHI CHI RODRIGUEZ

I'll drink to that.

JIMMY DEMARET AFTER A COLLEAGUE TOLD HIM HE'D WIN
MORE TOURNAMENTS IF HE EASED OFF ON THE BOTTLE

Scotland is the birthplace of
golf and salmon fishing. Which
may explain why it is also
the birthplace of whisky.

HENRY BEARD

———◦●●◦———

My players sank the white and
now I'm going to sink the black.

IAN WOOSNAM PROMISING TO DRINK SOME GUINNESS AFTER
HIS TEAM WON THE RYDER CUP IN IRELAND IN 2006

———◦●●◦———

In Ireland the 19th hole is
mandatory, as are 20 and 21.

BILL MURRAY

I once called his hotel room the morning after a convivial meeting. I said, 'Is that Lee Trevino?' A bleary voice answered, 'Wait a minute. Let me look in the mirror.'

GARY PLAYER

⎯⎯●●●⎯⎯

Somebody said once that every Irishman wanted to buy Christy O'Connor a drink – and that most had succeeded.

CHRISTY O'CONNOR

⎯⎯●●●⎯⎯

If you drink, don't drive. Don't even putt.

DEAN MARTIN

If you go to Ireland with a small hangover you'll come home with a big one.

SAM TORRANCE

———•●●•———

Doug Sanders only drinks socially now. He keeps a bottle of Socially in the clubhouse.

JOHN FORSYTHE

———•●●•———

'Greenkeeper, I dropped my bottle of Scotch out of the bag somewhere on the seventh. Anything handed in at lost-and-found?' 'Only the golfer who played after you, sir.'

ROBERT McCUNE

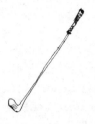

CLOTHES LINES

There's too much
fussiness in golf clubs.
I was asked to leave
my last one because
my socks weren't
colour coordinated
with my umbrella.

MILDRED SASSOON

They didn't wear Plus Fours
because they were crack players.
They were crack players because
they wore Plus Fours.

P. G. WODEHOUSE

———•••———

I had to change into brown
trousers after playing my
first hole at the Masters.

TREVOR HOMER

———•••———

I hope you're wearing
that for a bet.

COLIN MONTGOMERIE TO PAYNE STEWART

The golfing girl of today should indeed be grateful that she need not play in a sailor hat, a high stiff collar, a voluminous skirt and petticoats, a motor veil or a wide skirt with leather binding.

MABEL STRINGER

My gaad, I've got socks
older than you.

LEE TREVINO TO A 27-YEAR-OLD OPPONENT
AT A TOURNAMENT IN 1980

———•••———

Among Jimmy Demaret's
outfits was a 'golf tuxedo',
made without armpit seams
to allow for a free swing.

GEOFF TIBBALLS

———•••———

I have known girls to become
golfers as an excuse to
wear pink jumpers.

P. G. WODEHOUSE

Jackie Gleason once donated a sweater to a charity as a pro-am prize. Now there's a family of refugees living in it.

BOB HOPE

───●●───

The older I get, the less inclined I am to dress for golf as if for a polar expedition.

MICHAEL PARKINSON

───●●───

Palm Springs is a great golf town. They won't let you in unless you're wearing an alpaca sweater.

BOB HOPE

Although golf was originally restricted to wealthy, overweight Protestants, today it's open to anybody who owns hideous clothing.

DAVE BARRY

Azinger is wearing an all black outfit: black jumper, blue trousers, white shoes and a pink tea cosy hat.

RENTON LAIDLAW

'Play it as it lies' is one of the fundamental dictates of golf. The other is, 'Wear it if it clashes'.

HENRY BEARD

I wish they'd start talking
about the quality of my golf,
not my wardrobe. Print my
score, not my measurements.

CRAIG STADLER

It appears that Canadian golfers
are more laid-back than us Scots
about clothing. A club in British
Columbia has a sign which warns,
'No spikes on dance floor'.

TOM SHIELDS

Golf is not a sport. Golf is men
in ugly pants, walking.

ROSIE O'DONNELL

Doug Sanders' outfit has been described as looking like the aftermath of a direct hit on a pizza factory.

DAVE MARR

———•••———

George Burns looked perfect in his alpaca sweater, his knitted shirt and the best woods money could buy. What a pity he had to ruin it all by playing golf.

LLOYD MANGRUM

———•••———

I'd give up golf if I didn't have so many sweaters.

BOB HOPE

'Officer, I've just been knocked
down by my friend in a golf cart.'
'What gear was he in?'
'The usual woolly jumper
and Nike runners.'

LIAM O'MAHONY

———— •●• ————

I don't like playing in Scotland;
I can't swing the way I want
to wearing four sweaters, a
rain jacket and my pyjamas.

LEE TREVINO

HOT SHOTS

It must have been
the greatest four-
wood anyone ever hit.
It was so much on
the flag I had to lean
sideways to follow the
flight of the ball.

GARY PLAYER

There are days when you feel you
can't miss even when you try to.

JACK NICKLAUS

—•●•—

Golf shots aren't bullets,
they're arrows.

GREG NORMAN

—•●•—

All of us believe that our
good shots are the norm, and
our bad ones aberrations.

ALEC MORRISON

It was so good I
could nearly feel the
baby applauding.

A SEVEN-MONTHS-PREGNANT DONNA WHITE
AFTER A GOOD PUTT

I always had the feeling that the ground shook when Nick Faldo made contact with the ball.

DAVE CANNON

———•••———

My driving is so good these days I have to dial the operator long distance after I hit it.

LEE TREVINO

———•••———

A straight drive or a short chip stiff to the pin gives a player the bliss that used to come thinking of women, imagining if only he and she were alone on some island.

JOHN UPDIKE

GOLF TIPS

Golf tips are like
aspirin. One may do you
good, but if you swallow
the whole bottle you'll
be lucky to survive.

HARVEY PENICK

Never give up a hole. Quitting between tee and green is more habit-forming than drinking highballs before breakfast.

SAM SNEAD

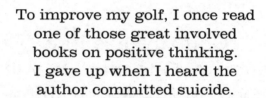

To improve my golf, I once read one of those great involved books on positive thinking. I gave up when I heard the author committed suicide.

NICK JOB

I tee the ball high because years of experience have shown me that air offers less resistance than dirt.

JACK NICKLAUS

The secret of missing a tree
is to aim straight for it.

MICHAEL GREEN

———— •●• ————

Never try to keep more than
300 separate thoughts in your
mind during your swing.

HENRY BEARD

———— •●• ————

Never break your putter and
your driver in the same round.

TOMMY BOLT

Relax into a rhythm that fits the hills and swales and play the shot at hand – not the last one, not the next one, but the one at your feet, in the poison ivy, where you put it.

JOHN UPDIKE

In his younger days, Andy Bean
developed a taste for snacking on
golf balls and wrestling alligators.
He might have been better
advised to swap things around.

GEOFF TIBBALLS

———•●●———

Drive for show, putt for dough.

ERNIE ELS

If you're making a deal with
a business associate on a golf
course, make sure you fine-
tune it before he tees off.
Particularly if you've got a
mortgage – or a heart condition.

TOM SMOTHERS

———◆●◆———

The best time to take up golf
is about ten years ago.

LESLIE NIELSEN

———◆●◆———

The secret of good golf is to play
it as though it were a game.

DOUG GAMBON

Take time to smell the flowers
on your way round.

WALTER HAGEN

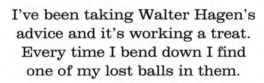

I've been taking Walter Hagen's
advice and it's working a treat.
Every time I bend down I find
one of my lost balls in them.

RUSS ABBOT

Hit it a bloody sight harder!

TED RAY AFTER A NOVICE ASKED HIM HOW HE
MIGHT GET THE BALL TO TRAVEL FURTHER

Never give another golfer
unsolicited advice, including
the advice to never give another
golfer unsolicited advice.

LESLIE NIELSEN

◆●●◆

Golf should never be played
on any day with a 'y' in it.

LES DAWSON

PRACTICE MAKES PERFECT

I have taught golf at a driving range for some time and have seen many people actually practising mistakes.

MEL FLANAGAN

I hate practice, my idea of
warming up is a double egg,
sausage, bacon and fried bread.

MICHAEL PARKINSON

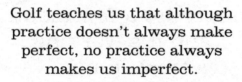

Golf teaches us that although
practice doesn't always make
perfect, no practice always
makes us imperfect.

TOM HARTMAN

I don't practise much these days.
At my age, you need to keep all
your energy for your actual shots.

SAM SNEAD AT 78

I've been practising
my swing in front of the
mirror for a few months
and it's working
a treat. I'm now
thoroughly proficient
at hitting... mirrors.

JOHN DENVER

They call me a natural player.
So why do I have to practise
till my hands bleed?

SEVE BALLESTEROS

• • •

Swinging at daisies is a bit like
playing the electric guitar with
a tennis racquet. If it were that
easy we could all be Jerry Garcia.
The ball changes everything.

MICHAEL BAMBERGER

• • •

All I know is I've seen Nicklaus
watch Hogan practise,
but I've never seen Hogan
watch Nicklaus practise.

TOMMY BOLT TO CHRISTY O'CONNOR AFTER BEING
ASKED TO COMPARE THE TWO GOLFERS

And then there was the
condemned golfer who asked
the hangman, 'Mind if I take
a few practice swings?'

HAL ROACH

———•◦•———

When Julius Boros putts, you
can't tell by looking whether
he's just practising or it's
fifty grand if he sinks it.

LEE TREVINO

———•◦•———

Are you girls practisin'
to come second?

FAMILIAR JEER FROM BABE ZAHARIAS TO HER OPPONENTS

LET'S PUTT IT LIKE THIS

Putting allows the
touchy golfer two to
four opportunities
to blow a gasket in
the short space of
two to 40 feet.

TOMMY BOLT

Whoever said putting
was a pleasure obviously
never played golf.

MICHAEL GREEN

———•••———

There are three things a man must
do alone: testify, die and putt.

BENNETT CERF

———•••———

I was putting like a
lobotomised baboon.

TONY JOHNSTON

The only time Clayton
Heafner could putt was when
he got mad enough to hate
the ball into the hole.

CARY MIDDLECOFF

———•●•———

The devoted golfer is an
anguished soul who has
learned a lot about putting,
just as an avalanche victim has
learned a lot about snow.

DAN JENKINS

———•●•———

The Coarse Golfer: one who has
to shout 'Fore' when he putts.

MICHAEL GREEN

Putt in haste and repent at leisure.

GERALD BATCHELOR

———•••———

A putt that's struck too hard
has only one way into the
cup – through the middle of
the front door. There's no
tradesman's entrance.

BOBBY JONES

———•••———

I think I know the answer to your
putting problems. You need to
hit the ball closer to the hole.

VALERIE HOGAN TO HER LEGENDARY HUSBAND BEN

81

WEIGHT WATCHERS

Golf and cricket are
the only two games
where you can actually
put on weight while
playing them.

TOMMY DOCHERTY

Some guys try to shoot their
age. Craig Stadler tries
to shoot his weight.

JIM MURRAY

———— •●• ————

The best way to lose weight
at golf is to go to a Mexican
course and drink the water.

BUDDY HACKETT

———— •●• ————

Corey Pavin looks like he was
in a famine. Craig Stadler
looks like he caused it.

ANDY WILLIAMS

Most of the guys on the tour are built like truck drivers but have the touch of hairdressers. Charlie Price is built like a hairdresser and he has the touch of a truck driver.

CLAYTON HEAFNER

It takes a lot of guts to play this game, and by looking at Billy Casper, you can tell he certainly has a lot.

GARY PLAYER

The fat bellies have slimmed down as the purses have grown fatter.

SAM TORRANCE

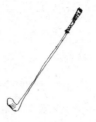

ER, COME AGAIN?

My 15 minutes
of fame ran to
almost a decade.

LAURA BAUGH

I'm learning not to get too excited after one good round and to keep my head on the ground.

COLIN MONTGOMERIE

Tenison was the hardest
easy course I ever played.

LEE TREVINO

Seve Ballesteros is relaxed
in an intense sort of way.

COLIN MONTGOMERIE

I would like to thank the press
from the heart of my bottom.

NICK FALDO AFTER WINNING THE OPEN IN 1992

Ballesteros felt much better today after a 69.

STEVE RYDER COMMENTING ON THE US MASTERS

———•●●———

95 per cent of putts which finish short don't go in.

ROBERT GREEN

———•●●———

Pinero has missed the putt. I wonder what he's thinking in Spanish.

RENTON LAIDLAW

Nick Faldo this afternoon is all
in blue, with a white shirt.

TONY ADAMSON

———•●•———

I would like to thank my parents –
especially my father and mother.

GREG NORMAN DURING HIS WINNING SPEECH AT THE
1983 WORLD MATCH PLAY CHAMPIONSHIP

———•●•———

I think I can just see the
corner of the ball.

JACK NEWTON

I must play less in order
to prolong my career.

SEVE BALLESTEROS

———— •◦• ————

I'm yesterday's man, or
rather I will be tomorrow.

PETER McEVOY

———— •◦• ————

This is Vicente Fernandez of
Argentina. You will notice that
he walks with a slight limp. This
is because he was born with one
leg shorter than the other two.

RODDY CARR WHILE COMMENTING ON THE IRISH OPEN

It would have been a birdie
if the ball hadn't stopped
before it reached the hole.

DAVID COLEMAN

If golf wasn't my living I
wouldn't play it if you paid me.

CHRISTY O'CONNOR

Hindsight is always 50/50.

CHARLIE DRAKE

So, Woosie, you're from Wales.
What part of Scotland is that?

AMERICAN JOURNALIST TO IAN WOOSNAM
DURING A 1987 PRESS CONFERENCE

———•••———

Gary Player had to be a better
golfer than Jack Nicklaus
in order to be as good.

PETER DOBEREINER

THE FEMALE OF
THE SPECIES

If it wasn't for golf,
I'd probably be the fat
lady in the circus now.

KATHY WHITWORTH

I achieved a lot by climbing over
113 golfers. The only problem was
that there were 114 ahead of me.

JOANNE CARNER AFTER SECURING THE RUNNERS-UP
SPOT IN THE U.S. WOMEN'S OPEN, HAVING RECOVERED
FROM 115TH PLACE AFTER THE FIRST ROUND

———•••———

If a woman can walk,
she can play golf.

LOUISE SUGGS

———•••———

I'd like to see Bo Derek
after 18 holes in 100-degree
weather. Those cornrows and
beads would be history.

JAN STEPHENSON

My driving style? I
just loosen my girdle
and let her rip.

BABE ZAHARIAS

I'll take a two-shot penalty, but I'll be damned if I'm going to play the ball where it lies.

ELAINE JOHNSON IN 1982 AFTER HER TEE-SHOT REBOUNDED OFF A TREE AND ENDED UP IN HER BRA

HOLES-IN-ONE

If your opponent in a money match gets a hole-in-one shortly after he tells you he hasn't played the game in months, count your fingers after he shakes hands with you.

JACKIE GLEASON

I don't believe in George Bush, the tooth fairy and guys who get holes-in-one when nobody is looking.

RICH HALL

Always tell the truth. You may make a hole-in-one when you're alone on the golf course some day.

FRANKLIN P. JONES

All golfers blame chance for other accidents, but accept full responsibility when they hit a hole-in-one.

ALAN BLACKWELL

Last week I missed a spectacular hole-in-one by only five strokes.

BOB HOPE

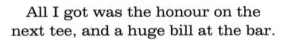

All I got was the honour on the next tee, and a huge bill at the bar.

VAUGHAN SOMERS ON THE HOLE-IN-ONE WHICH WON HIM THE SURFER'S PARADISE TOURNAMENT IN 1981

It's a pity I don't have a video of the hole-in-one I once made, but they weren't invented then.

BOB MONKHOUSE

Did you hear about the golfer
who killed the Puerto Rican?
He shot a hole in Juan.

ROY 'CHUBBY' BROWN

———— •●● ————

The club grouch was unhappy
about everything: the food,
the assessments, the parking,
the other members. The first
time he hit a hole-in-one he
complained. 'Damn it – just when
I needed the putting practice!'

JOEY ADAMS

PREFERRED LIES

Question on golf
etiquette: What do you
do when your opponent
claims to have found
his ball in the rough,
and you know he's a
liar because you've got
it in your pocket?

GEORGE COOTE

Truth is something you leave in
the locker room with your street
shoes when you play golf.

TERRY MARTIN

⎯⎯⎯●●⎯⎯⎯

In golf the ball usually lies
poorly, and the player well.

WILLIAM DAVIES

⎯⎯⎯●●⎯⎯⎯

A lie is either where the ball
has come to rest or where the
player claims it came to rest.

PETER GAMMOND

Golfers start by excusing poor shots by claiming bad lies. With time, such lies improve dramatically.

CHEVY CHASE

Nothing handicaps you so much in golf as honesty.

OLIVER CRONIN

The one reward golf has given me, and I shall always be thankful for it, is introducing me to some of the world's most picturesque, tireless and bald-faced liars.

RING LARDNER

MAGNIFICENT OBSESSION

There are only two
types of people in the
world: golfers and non-
golfers. Once bitten,
it is akin to having
your neck punctured in
Transylvania – there
is no known antidote.

MARTIN JOHNSON

Golf is my profession.
Show business is just to
pay the green fees.

BOB HOPE

Real golfers go to work to relax.

GEORGE DILLON

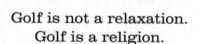

Golf is not a relaxation.
Golf is a religion.

BOB REID

I'll play golf until I die, and
then I want them to roll me into
a bunker, cover me with sand
and make sure nobody's ball
lands in there for a while.

LEE TREVINO

———— •••• ————

The reason golf obsesses so
many is that it answers a
latent lunacy in its devotees, or
perhaps by its frustrations and
impossibilities tips them into one.

A. C. GRAYLING

Golfers are a level-headed lot. They only talk about golf three times a day: before they play, while they're playing and after they've played.

KATHARINE WHITEHORN

* * *

What is love compared to holing out before your opponent?

P. G. WODEHOUSE

* * *

You know you're a bit weird when you ask for *Golf Digest* bedtime stories at three.

JOHN ELLIS

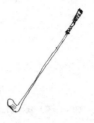

CONUNDRUMS

How is it that a man can push a lawnmower for an hour and call it work, but when he pushes a golf cart all day he calls it recreation?

Why is it called a three-wood
when it's made out of metal?

ERNIE WITHAM

―――――•●•―――――

If the universe is finite, as people
say, how come golfers never
find all the balls they lose?

HAL ROACH

―――――•●•―――――

Do golfers' drives put them crazy
or their putts drive them crazy?

VALERIE FERGUSON

Is it any accident that 'God' comes just before 'golf' in the dictionary?

DAVE ALLEN

If golf is a rich man's game, how come there are so many poor players?

MITCH MURRAY

The true secret of golf is: One day you play really well and the next really crap – and you don't know why.

PATRICK RAYNER

THE UNKINDEST CUTS OF ALL

When Paul Azinger
turned professional in
1981 it was as though
the village idiot had
just announced his
intention to pursue a
career in astrophysics.

BILL ELLIOT

A nice old lady with a
croquet mallet could have
saved him two strokes.

BERNARD DARWIN ON BOBBY JONES' PITIFUL
DISPLAY AT THE BRITISH OPEN IN 1930

Deane Beman couldn't hit the
ball out of his own shadow.

PETER ALLISS

You don't have to keep score when
you play golf with Jerry Ford.
You just look back along the
fairway and follow the wounded.

BOB HOPE

Anything that moves
– and everything
that's nailed down
– has a sponsor.

MIRIAM LORD ON THE RYDER CUP

I've got an attachment for Lee Trevino. It fits over his mouth.

JACK NICKLAUS

———•••———

Few people are sensible about holidays. Many play golf, and one odd effect of that pursuit is that they return to work manifestly stupider than they were. It is, I think, the company of other golfers.

G. W. LYTTELTON

———•••———

Arnold Palmer turned golf into a game of 'hit it hard, go find it and hit it again'.

JOHN SCHULIAN

What's the difference between
Gordon Bland and a coconut?
You can get a drink
out of a coconut.

SIMON HOBDAY

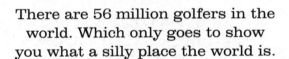

There are 56 million golfers in the
world. Which only goes to show
you what a silly place the world is.

KENNY LYNCH

When we arrive you can see the
secretary flicking through the
book and thinking, 'Why have
these guys turned up? No one
ordered a taxi or a takeaway'.

ASIAN OPEN CHAIRMAN JAZ ATHWAL ON RACISM IN GOLF

Colin Montgomerie walks round a golf course like a man under the impression that smiling gives you herpes.

LAWRENCE DONEGAN

———◆●◆———

Europe did their best to help America win the Ryder Cup in 2006. We picked Ian Woosnam as captain.

OLIVER HOLT

———◆●◆———

I wouldn't recommend golf to my worst enemy. Actually on second thoughts I would.

JOHN WAYNE

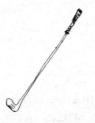

SELF-ABUSE

I'm into golf now. I'm getting pretty good. I can almost hit the ball as far as I can throw the clubs.

BOB ETTINGER

My most notable trait is snatching
defeat out of the jaws of victory.

DOUG SAUNDERS

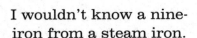

I wouldn't know a nine-
iron from a steam iron.

LISE HAND

I'm a solid player apart from
a drink problem, the yips and
a tendency to break my clubs
every time I hit a bad shot.

SIMON HOBDAY

I call golf 'Connect the sand traps'. I can play four or five rounds without having the ball touch grass once.

JACK BENNY

———◦●●◦———

My game's gone off so much that when I went fishing a couple of weeks ago my first cast missed the lake.

BEN CRENSHAW IN 1977

I don't rent golf carts. I don't
need them. Where I hit the ball,
I can use public transportation.

GENE PERRET

———•◦•———

Maybe I should go to a sports
shop and buy a trophy. That's the
only way I'm going to get one.

SEVE BALLESTEROS DURING A BAD SPELL IN HIS CAREER

———•◦•———

Spell 'golf' backwards and
you have a pretty good idea
of my playing style.

GEORGE BURNS

I played so badly I got a get-well card from the Inland Revenue.

JOHNNY MILLER IN 1977

———•••———

I tried to play like Jack Nicklaus, but ended up more like Jacques Tati.

DAVID FEHERTY AFTER A POOR DISPLAY IN 1992

———•••———

It took me 17 years to get 3,000 hits in baseball. I did the same thing in one afternoon on the golf course.

HANK AARON

We couldn't hit a cow's
arse with a banjo.

MARK JAMES ON THE RYDER CUP TEAM IN 1977

Golf.

JACKIE GLEASON AFTER BEING ASKED
WHAT HIS HANDICAP WAS

———•●•———

I play golf like Cinderella. I
never make it to the ball.

DON RICKLES

———•●•———

You learn a lot about yourself
by playing golf. Unfortunately,
most of it is unprintable.

BURT LANCASTER

I was reading the other day that
there are 2,000 different ways
you can hit the ball wrong. So far
I think I've reached about 1,800.

DINAH SHORE

———•●●•———

My career started slowly,
then tapered off.

GARY McCORD

———•●●•———

If my IQ had been two points
lower I'd have been a plant.

LEE TREVINO

HERE'S TO THE LOSERS

The only thing I ever
learned from losing
was that I don't like it.

TOM WATSON

Few things draw two men
together more than a mutual
inability to play golf.

P. G. WODEHOUSE

———•••———

Defeat is worse than
death, because you have
to live with defeat.

NICK FALDO

———•••———

I find it more satisfying to be a
bad player at golf. The worse you
play, the better you remember
the occasional good shot.

NUBAR GULBENKIAN

Golf is popular because it is the best game in the world at which to be bad. It is, after all, the bad player who gets the most strokes.

A. A. MILNE

—•●•—

I never liked team sports because it annoyed me that if you did your bit you could still go home a loser.

NICK FALDO

—•●•—

Show me a good loser and I'll show you a loser.

GARY PLAYER

CADDYSHACK

The first thing to
understand about
caddying is that it's
not brain surgery.
It's much more
complicated than that.

LAWRENCE DONEGAN

Players make mistakes.
Caddies make blunders.

JERRY OSBORNE

* * *

After his last shot, Mr Smith
turned to his caddy and asked,
'What did you think of my game?'
The caddy thought for a moment
and then replied, 'Quite good,
sir, but I prefer golf myself.'

KEVIN GOLDSTEIN-JACKSON

* * *

I once sank a 35-yard putt against
Billy Graham. When I turned
round I saw my caddy had been
turned into a pillar of salt.

BOB HOPE

Divorces between caddies and players are often executed on the spot, and there isn't any alimony.

JOHN O'REILLY

———•●•———

Golfer to caddy after messing up a shot: Golf is a funny old game, innit? Caddy: The way you play it it certainly is, sir.

GREG DOHERTY

———•●•———

A bunch of bums who whistle through their teeth, don't know which club to put into my hand, and smell strongly of BO, alcohol or both.

SAM SNEAD ON THE ST ANDREWS CADDIES

I never kick my ball in the rough
or improve my lie in a sand
trap. For that I have a caddy.

BOB HOPE

Real golfers, no matter what the
provocation, never strike a caddy
with the driver. The sand wedge
is infinitely more effective.

HUXTABLE PIPPEY

I asked Marilyn Monroe if she'd
come golfing with me one day.
'I can't,' she said, 'I don't even
know how to hold the caddy.'

DEAN MARTIN

If each time a player and caddy split up was actually a divorce, most tour players would have been married more times than Zsa Zsa Gabor and Liz Taylor combined.

PETER JACOBSEN

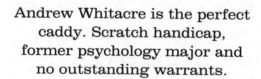

Andrew Whitacre is the perfect caddy. Scratch handicap, former psychology major and no outstanding warrants.

BILL MURRAY

There were three things in the world that he held in the smallest esteem: slugs, poets and caddies with hiccups.

P. G. WODEHOUSE

And then there was the golfer who said to her caddy, 'Notice any improvement today, Jack?' And Jack replies, 'Yes, ma'am, I see you got your hair done.'

STUART WHITLEY

I asked my caddy if I had a shot to the green. He replied, 'Mr Murray, I would say you have several shots to the green.'

IAN MURRAY

After bumping four balls into the rough on the spin, I asked my caddy what I should take for my next shot. 'Either a cyanide capsule,' he replied, 'or the next plane home.'

JACK LEMMON

ODIOUS COMPARISONS

Colin Montgomerie
has a face like a
warthog that's been
stung by a wasp.

DAVID FEHERTY

Ballesteros goes after a golf course
the way a lion goes after a cobra.

JIM MURRAY

———•●•———

Golf is like love or the measles.
You're better off if you get
over it early in life.

G. K. CHESTERTON

———•●•———

My golfing career? On one hole
I'm like Arnold Palmer, and then
at the next I'm Lilli Palmer.

SEAN CONNERY

Every time Padraig Harrington
hits a great shot he looks like
a wino who's just found a
tenner in his inside pocket.

LAWRENCE DONEGAN

———•●●•———

I once made an effort to master
elephant polo in Delhi. It was a bit
like playing golf with a fishing rod.

MAX BOYCE

———•●●•———

In 1991 Tom Sieckman won the
Philippine Open, the Thailand
Open and the Singapore Open,
leaving him second only to the US
Marines for victories in the Pacific.

GARY NUHM

Golf balls are attracted to water as unerringly as the eye of a middle-aged man to a female bosom.

MICHAEL GREEN

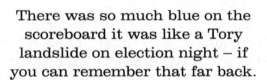

There was so much blue on the scoreboard it was like a Tory landslide on election night – if you can remember that far back.

OLIVER HOLT ON EUROPE'S DECISIVE VICTORY OVER AMERICA IN THE 2006 RYDER CUP

Ballesteros's form is up and down more often than a whore's knickers.

OLIVER HORNSBY

The difference between a good golf shot and a bad one is the same as the difference between a beautiful and a plain woman – a matter of millimetres.

IAN FLEMING

Corey Pavin plays golf as if he were double-parked and left the meter running. Guys move slower leaving hotel fires.

JIM MURRAY

Asking Jack Nicklaus to re-design Augusta was like asking Andy Warhol to re-paint the Sistine Chapel.

DAVID FEHERTY

He took a swing like a man with a wasp under his shirt and his pants on fire, trying to impale a butterfly on the end of a scythe.

PAUL GALLICO

To say I was disappointed would be like saying Custer had a spot of bother at Little Bighorn.

TONY JACKLIN AFTER POOR WEATHER AND A HECKLER UPSET HIS PLAY AT ST ANDREWS

In ancient Egypt when the pharaohs died, forceps were inserted through their nostrils to pull their brains down from their skulls. I feel roughly the same sensation when I watch golf.

KEVIN MYERS

PUTTERING OUT

You can take a man's
wife. You can even
take his wallet. But
never on any account
take his putter.

ARCHIE COMPSTON

The less said about
the putter the better.
It is an instrument of
torture, designed by
Tantalus and forged in
the devil's own smithy.

TONY LEMA

In my house in Houston I still have the putter with which I missed that 2½-foot putt to win the Open. It's in two pieces.

DOUG SANDERS

———•◦•———

When you're putting well you're a good putter. When your opponent is putting well he has a good putter.

JOHN D. SHERIDAN

Tommy Bolt's putters spent more time in the air than Lindbergh.

JIMMY DEMARET ON THE TEMPERAMENTAL AMERICAN

———•●•———

When you're putting well you can't hear anything off the green. but when you're putting badly you can hear a man jingle two coins in his pocket 100 yards away.

TONY JACKLIN

———•●•———

Lee Trevino's patter is better than his putter.

NICK LUNDBERG

My putter worked so well for me today I'm going to sleep with it tonight. My husband will have to go next door.

JOANNE CARNER

Do that again and you'll wear my putter.

BOB SHEARER TO A PHOTOGRAPHER WHO DISTRACTED HIM WHILE PLAYING A SHOT IN 1975

I find it helpful to inform an opponent who's lining up a four-foot putt that under the metric system widely used in other countries, it's actually a putt of just over 1,200 millimetres.

LESLIE NIELSEN

WATCH YOUR LANGUAGE

Golf is the easiest
game in the world to
play. You just hit the
ball and then swear.

SID CAESAR

I don't like people asking me if I golf. Using 'golf' as a verb is a bit like using sex as one. Would you say to somebody, 'Do you sex?'

DAVID OWEN

———•••———

The finest golfers are the least loquacious.

P. G. WODEHOUSE

———•••———

No problem, Greg. You don't need to talk. Just listen.

LEE TREVINO TO AN EXASPERATED GREG NORMAN WHO SAID TO HIM, 'DO YOU MIND IF WE DON'T TALK DURING THE GAME TODAY?'

Conversation interferes with most people's golf. With Lee Trevino, golf interferes with his conversations.

RETIEF GOOSEN

———•●•———

A Shi'ite effort.

DAVID FEHERTY ON A POOR SHOT HE PLAYED IN THE DUBAI DESERT CLASSIC

———•●•———

Sean doesn't enjoy his golf as much since he had his operation. He can't swear as much.

SEAN CONNERY'S WIFE AFTER HE HAD LASER SURGERY ON HIS THROAT IN 1992

I don't know why people say
Ben Hogan is untalkative. He
speaks to me on every green.
He says, 'You're away.'

JIMMY DEMARET

———•••———

It is embarrassing for me to
play on the US circuit. I once
asked my caddy for a sand
wedge and he came back ten
minutes later with ham on rye.

CHI CHI RODRIGUEZ

WHAT'S YOUR HANDICAP?

Handicaps are allocations of strokes that permit players of very different ability to do equally poorly on the same golf course.

HENRY BEARD

My caddy.

WALTER TRAVIS ON BEING ASKED WHAT HIS HANDICAP WAS

Talk about handicap —
I'm a one-eyed Negro Jew.

SAMMY DAVIS JR

Like all 24-handicap men,
Fisher had the most perfect
confidence in his ability to beat
all other 24-handicap men.

P. G. WODEHOUSE

'What is your handicap?' Lady Cunard asked Lord Castlerose on the golf course. 'Drink and debauchery,' he answered sadly but truthfully.

PHILIP ZIEGLER

The great thing about the handicap is that a guy who can't break 100 can kick the shit out of Phil Mickelson.

JOHN DALY

I always play golf with a handy cap on my head.

LES DAWSON

LET'S GO CLUBBING

Most new sets of golf
clubs still include three-
irons, even though most
regular golfers would
get more use from a
second umbrella.

DAVID OWEN

I once gave a lesson about clubs. After it was over, a lady informed me she knew how to recognise a six-iron: there were six holes in the top of the grip.

MEL FLANAGAN

I see dots

Buddy Hackett and Jimmy Durante were once playing golf and Durante was having a particularly bad game, his score well over 200. At the end he asked Hackett what he should give his caddy. 'Your clubs,' Hackett replied.

DES LYNAM

The trouble about
getting a new set of
clubs is that if you're
still playing crap
you have nothing
to blame it on.

BEN ELTON

COURSES FROM HELL

There's nothing wrong
with St Andrews
that 100 bulldozers
couldn't put right.

ED FURGOL

When the wind blows at St
Andrews, even the seagulls walk.

NICK FALDO

———●●———

In the rough at Muirfield not
only could you lose your golf
ball, but if you left your golf bag
down you could lose that too. You
could even lose a short caddy.

JACK NICKLAUS

———●●———

The 13th at St Andrews is a great
hole. It gives you a million options,
not one of them worth a damn.

TOM KITE

Visiting St Andrews is like
visiting your old grandmother.
She's crotchety and eccentric
but also elegant, and anyone
who doesn't fall in love with
her has no imagination.

NICK FALDO

———•••———

If you're standing on the first tee
at Sotogrande and you can see
Gibraltar, rain is on the way. If you
can't, it's already pissing down.

ERIC SYKES

———•••———

I saw Edmund Hillary at
Sawgrass – and he was having a
hard time keeping his balance.

TOM WEISKOPF

Columbus went round the world
in 1492. That's pretty good
considering the size of the course.

MILTON BERLE

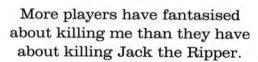

More players have fantasised
about killing me than they have
about killing Jack the Ripper.

COURSE DESIGNER ROBERT TRENT JONES, WHO WAS
RENOWNED FOR HIS 'SADISTIC' COURSES

Peter Dye used so much
wood, his courses may be the
first ever to burn down.

BARRY McDERMOTT ON THE FAMOUS ARCHITECT

Golf is a cruel game anyway, so
why should I design courses fairly?

PETER DYE

A golf course is comprised of 18
holes, 17 of them unnecessary,
but included simply to create the
maximum amount of frustration.

TERRY WOGAN

All Hazeltine needs is 80
acres and some cows.

DAVE HILL

LET'S GET PHYSICAL

Golf groupies must be
the most passive of
any competitive game.
Even chess fans display
greater vivacity.

ROBERT O'BYRNE

I wish it had bitten me
a little lower down.

DAVID FEHERTY, WHOSE ARM SWELLED UP
TO TWICE ITS NORMAL SIZE AFTER BEING
BITTEN BY A SNAKE AT WENTWORTH

My wife gave me ten oysters
last night to rouse my passion,
but only nine of them worked.

LEE TREVINO

———————•●●•———————

A true pro always prefers his
golf course to his intercourse.

CONAN O'BRIEN

———————•●●•———————

Would you say a golfer is a
man who putts it about?

BEN ELTON

THE ICONS

Nick Faldo's idea of excitement is having his After Eight mints at 7.30.

GRAHAM ELLIOTT

Seve Ballesteros hits
the ball farther than
I go on my holidays.

LEE TREVINO

I've had a bad week. But in
the real world a bad week is
waking up and finding you're
a steelworker in Scunthorpe.

NICK FALDO

———•••———

Jack Nicklaus is a legend
in his spare time.

TOM WATSON

———•••———

They keep talking about the
Big Four – Palmer, Nicklaus,
Player and Trevino. I just
want to be the fifth wheel in
case somebody gets a flat.

CHI CHI RODRIGUEZ

I don't have an image or a nickname. Maybe I should dye my hair peroxide blonde and call myself The Great White Tadpole.

IAN WOOSNAM

———•••———

Tiger Woods has such a lazy style, last week I caught him nodding off on his backswing.

VALERIE NETTER

———•••———

Sam Snead has a terrific pair of legs. He's double-jointed. He can stand flat-footed in a room and kick an 8-foot ceiling.

LEE TREVINO

John Daly could draw a
crowd in Saskatchewan.

ROCCO MEDIATE

———•◦•———

Arnold Palmer would go
for the flag from the middle
of an alligator's back.

LEE TREVINO

———•◦•———

Knock knock.
Who's there?
Tiger.
Tiger who?
Ah, the fickleness of fame.

ANONYMOUS

PERENNIAL LAWS
OF THE GAME

A golf ball will always
travel furthest when hit
in the wrong direction.

HENRY BEARD

Most good shots are accidents.

EUGENE BLACK

He who swisheth most,
driveth least.

MICHAEL GREEN

Every golfer knows that a
ball only bounces off a tree
in the direction of the hole if
there's a bunker in the way.

SID CAESAR

The number of tees in your
bag is always less than
3 or more than 600.

MICHAEL RYAN

———•••———

Golf gifts given to us by non-
golfers are invariably useless.

SERGIO GARCIA

———•••———

Golf is all about preparation.
First you get your clubs,
then you rehearse your
excuses, then you play.

PHIL SILVERS

SENIOR CITIZENS

I know exactly when
I want to retire now,
but when I reach that
time I may not.

JACK NICKLAUS

People ask me why I still
play golf at my age. I have to.
I'm too old for marbles and
too married for women.

BOB HOPE

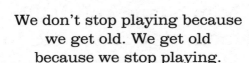

We don't stop playing because
we get old. We get old
because we stop playing.

WALTER HAGEN

One of the nice things about the
Senior Tour is that we can take a
cart and a cooler. If your game isn't
going well, you can have a picnic.

LEE TREVINO

Men chase golf balls
when they're too old to
chase anything else.

GROUCHO MARX

BYE BYE BIRDIE

My boss told me I needed to de-stress myself so he suggested golf. It was a very wise suggestion. I gave it up.

BEN CABOT

He enjoys that perfect peace,
that peace beyond all human
understanding, that peace which
cometh at its maximum only to
a man who has given up golf.

P. G. WODEHOUSE

———•••———

I gave up golf for painting because
it takes me less strokes.

DWIGHT D. EISENHOWER

When I retire I'm going to get a pair of grey slacks, a white shirt, a striped tie, a blue blazer and a case of dandruff and go stand on the first tee so I can be a USGA official.

LEE TREVINO

That was a great game of golf, fellas.

BING CROSBY'S REPUTED LAST WORDS

I'm fed up of reading about retired tennis players taking up golf. When I retire, I'm going to take up tennis.

JIMMY DEMARET

———•—•—•———

It's time to give up golf when birds flying south readjust their flight patterns to let you hit.

RICHARD MIZINER

THE LAST LAUGH

I have often been
gratefully aware of
the heroic efforts of
my opponents not
to laugh at me.

BERNARD DARWIN

While the ethics of golf forbid coughing, talking, sneering, snoring or making any other sort of noise while our opponent addresses the ball, it is not illegal to throw flares or tickle his ears with a wisp of straw.

RING LARDNER

●—●●—●

He seemed to be attempting to deceive his ball and lull it into a false sense of security by looking away from it and then making a lightning slash in the apparent hope of catching it off its guard.

P. G. WODEHOUSE

If you're interested in finding out more about our books, find us on Facebook at **Summersdale Publishers** and follow us on Twitter at **@Summersdale**.

www.summersdale.com